I Know the Rules!

I HELP CLEAN UP!

By Bray Jacobson

Gareth Stevens
PUBLISHING

Please visit our website, www.garethstevens.com. For a free color catalog of all our high-quality books, call toll free 1-800-542-2595 or fax 1-877-542-2596.

Library of Congress Cataloging-in-Publication Data

Names: Jacobson, Bray, author.
Title: I help clean up! / Bray Jacobson.
Description: Buffalo, New York : Gareth Stevens Publishing, [2024] |
  Series: I know the rules! | Includes index.
Identifiers: LCCN 2022051454 (print) | LCCN 2022051455 (ebook) | ISBN
  9781538286593 (Library Binding) | ISBN 9781538286586 (Paperback) | ISBN
  9781538286609 (eBook)
Subjects: LCSH: Cleaning–Juvenile literature.
Classification: LCC TX324 .J33 2023 (print) | LCC TX324 (ebook) | DDC
  648–dc23/eng/20221115
LC record available at https://lccn.loc.gov/2022051454
LC ebook record available at https://lccn.loc.gov/2022051455

Published in 2024 by
Gareth Stevens Publishing
2544 Clinton Street
Buffalo, NY 14224

Copyright © 2024 Gareth Stevens Publishing

Designer: Claire Wrazin
Editor: Kristen Nelson

Photo credits: Cover, p. 1 Pixel-Shot/Shutterstock.com; p. 5 Lukassek/Shutterstock.com; pp. 7, 9 wavebreakmedia/Shutterstock.com; p. 11 JOKE_PHATRAPONG/Shutterstock.com; p. 13 MNStudio/Shutterstock.com; pp. 15, 17 Evgeny Atamanenko/Shutterstock.com; pp. 19, 21 ezhenaphoto/Shutterstock.com; p. 23 sivilla/Shutterstock.com; p. 24 (left) otnaydur/Shutterstock.com; p. 24 (middle) Yuganov Konstantin/Shutterstock.com; p. 24 (right) donatas1205/Shutterstock.com.

All rights reserved. No part of this book may be reproduced in any form without permission in writing from the publisher, except by a reviewer.

Printed in the United States of America

CPSIA compliance information: Batch #CSGS24: For further information contact Gareth Stevens, at 1-800-542-2595.

Contents

School Clean Up 4

Cleaning Up at Home . . . 12

Toy Mess! 18

Words to Know 24

Index 24

I help clean up.
It is a rule at school.

Lucas paints at art time.
He uses many colors.
It gets messy!

Lucas helps clean up.
He washes his hands.
He puts the paint away.

Trish takes books off the shelf.
She reads them.
She puts them back!

I help clean up at home.

Grandma and Kelvin baked cookies.

They washed the dishes.
They wiped the counter.
They cleaned up together!

Joannie played with blocks.
She made a tower.

She put her blocks away.
She cleaned up!

How can you help clean up?

Words to Know

 dishes

 paint

 shelf

Index

art, 6
bake, 14

put away, 8, 10, 20
wash, 8, 16